Contents

Introduction   4

Papier-mâché Tambourine   6

Shake, Rattle and Roll   8

Shoe-box Guitar   10

Pop Star   12

Drum Away   14

Kazoo Band   16

Ping-pong Conductor   18

Hosepipe Panpipes   20

Thumb Piano   22

Pop-up Singer   24

Bottle Xylophone   26

The Orchestra   28

Glossary   30

Resources   31

Index   32

Intr uction

In this book you can learn about music and musical instruments both by reading about them and by having fun with craft activities. The information in the fact boxes will tell you about instruments from all over the world - their history, how they are used and what they are made of. You will learn something about modern music too, including rock music's favourite instrument - the guitar.

Do you know how an orchestra is made up? At the end of the book is a plan to show the different sections of an orchestra, the instruments each section contains, and where all the different players sit. There is also a list of places to visit if you want to find out more.

But now you can get your fingers sticky - making musical instruments as you read about them. Then you can make your own music!

MUSIC

Ting and Neil Morris

Illustrated by Ruth Levy

FRANKLIN WATTS
LONDON·SYDNEY

This symbol appears on some pages throughout this book. It indicates that adult supervision is advisable for that activity.

This edition published in 2004 by
Franklin Watts
96 Leonard Street
London
EC2A 4XD

Franklin Watts Australia
45-51 Huntley Street
Alexandria
NSW 2015

Cover design: Alice Young
Editor: Hazel Poole
Consultant: David Lambert
Designer: Sally Boothroyd
Photography: John Butcher
Artwork: Ruth Levy / Joanne Cowne
Models: Emma Morris
Picture Research: Ambreen Husain

ISBN 0 7496 5909 2

A CIP catalogue record is available for this book at the British Library.

Equipment and material

The projects in this book provide an introduction to the use of different art and craft media, and need little adult help. Most of the objects are made with throwaway household "junk" such as boxes, plastic bottles and containers, newspaper and fabric remnants. Paints, brushes, glues and modelling materials will have to be bought, but if stored correctly will last for a long time and for many more craft activities.

In this book the following materials are used:

bamboo sticks
beads
biscuit tin
braid (gold)
brushes (for glue and paint)
cardboard tubes
cellophane
cloth tape (coloured)
corks
craft knife
curtain rings
cutting board
dowel rods
dry peas, beans or lentils
fabric (scraps)
felt (scraps)
felt pens
foil (coloured)
foil dishes
garden rods or sticks
glass bottles
glue (water-based PVA, which can be used for thickening paint and as a varnish; strong glue such as UHU for sticking plastic, metal and fabric; glue stick)

hammer
hosepipe
jar (for mixing paint and paste)
jug
labels (sticky)
lids
lolly sticks
metal nuts and washers
nails
paint (powder, acrylic, ready-mixed or poster paints)
paper (thick and thin card; greaseproof paper; tissue paper; newspaper; sugar paper; cartridge paper)
pasta shapes
pencils
pencil sharpener
ping-pong balls
plastic bottle
plasticine
plywood
ribbon

rope
rubber bands
ruler
sandpaper
scissors
shirt (old)
shoe box
stapler
straws
string
tacks
tape (sticky tape; parcel tape; masking tape)
tape measure
toothpicks
varnish (PVA mixed with cold water)
wallpaper paste (fungicide-free)
washing-up liquid bottle
water
wood
wool
yoghurt pots

Papier-mâché Tambourine

Here's a good way to get into the rhythm!

1 Start by tearing newspaper into 2-cm squares. Then mix the wallpaper paste as instructed on the packet.

YOU WILL NEED:
✓card ✓stapler ✓newspaper ✓fungicide-free wallpaper paste
✓PVA glue ✓yellow poster paint ✓ready-mixed paint
✓curtain rings ✓metal washers ✓beads ✓string ✓rubber band
✓tissue paper ✓cellophane or greaseproof paper ✓scissors
✓brushes (for glue and paint) ✓water

2 To make the frame of the tambourine, cut a strip of card 65 cm x 6 cm. Bend the strip into a circle, overlap the ends and staple them together.

3 Cover both sides of the frame with a layer of wallpaper paste. Then press newspaper squares into the paste, smoothing out air bubbles and pushing the pieces together with your fingers. Then apply another layer of paste and newspaper squares. Add two further layers to the outside of the frame, pasting down any newspaper that is sticking over the top edge. Make sure the frame is bent into its circular shape and allow it to dry for a few hours.

4 Now turn the frame over to do the bottom edge. Apply one more layer of paste and newspaper to the inside and three more layers to the outside. Make sure that the bottom edge is even and that all the newspaper is turned in and pasted down. Check again that the frame is nice and round, and then let it dry. This will take a few days.

5 When the frame is completely dry, ask an adult to make six pairs of holes as shown, large enough for string to pass through.

6 Give the frame an undercoat of ready mixed paint before painting the whole thing yellow.

7 When the paint has dried, you can decorate the frame. Twist strips of tissue paper together and roll pieces into little balls. Dilute PVA glue with some water to a creamy consistency and soak the decorations in it before sticking them in position. Then varnish the frame with diluted PVA.

8 Cut six short pieces of string and thread a number of metal washers, curtain rings and beads on each. Push the ends of the string through the pairs of holes, and knot the string inside the frame.

The tambourine

The tambourine is a simple percussion instrument - that is, it makes a sound when it is struck or shaken. The main sound is made by hitting skin or plastic stretched over a wooden or metal hoop. There are also metal discs set in the frame, which jingle when the tambourine is shaken. Sometimes players rub their thumb around the edge to make a jingling sound. The tambourine is a very old instrument. Ancient carvings show tambourines that look similar to the ones we know. Today this instrument is widely used by the dancers of Spain and Latin America, and sometimes by pop groups.

9 If you want to add a skin to your tambourine, stretch a piece of cellophane or greaseproof paper over the frame. Secure it tightly with a rubber band, and carefully cut off the overlapping edges. Now you can rattle and drum!

Shake, Rattle and Roll

1 Take two yoghurt pots. Put a handful of dry beans into one pot. Then join the two pots together with masking tape. Shake them to make sure you are happy with the sound.

YOU WILL NEED:
- ✔ 2 identical yoghurt pots
- ✔ 2 identical foil dishes
- ✔ washing-up liquid bottle
- ✔ stick ✔ dry peas, beans or lentils
- ✔ masking tape ✔ stapler ✔ coloured foil ✔ pasta shapes
- ✔ poster paint ✔ acrylic paint ✔ ribbon ✔ PVA glue
- ✔ brushes (for glue and paint)

2 Glue on some strips of coloured foil to decorate your shaker.

3 Paint small pasta shapes with thick poster paint. Cover the ends of the shaker with a layer of PVA glue and press the shapes into it. When it is dry, varnish the shapes with a second layer of glue.

4 Make another shaker with foil dishes. First put in a mixture of peas and beans to vary the sound. Unfold the edges of the dishes and staple them together.

5 Decorate the sides with painted pasta shapes, peas and lentils. Use plenty of PVA glue to hold the decorations in position. Then glue a wide ribbon around the stapled edges.

Maracas

Maracas belong to a family of musical instruments called idiophones. These are instruments made of materials that naturally make a sound when they are struck or shaken. Other idiophones are the xylophone, cymbals, castanets and triangle.

Maracas are instruments that you shake to make a rattling sound. They were originally made from the dried hollow shell of a gourd, which is a large fruit. This contained dried seeds or beans that could rattle about inside, and was attached to a handle. Maracas originated in Latin America, where they are used mainly in dance bands to give a strong rhythm. They are usually played in pairs.

Today maracas are often made of plastic and have lead shot inside, which gives a stronger sound.

6 You could add a rattle with a handle to your shaker collection. Pull the nozzle off an empty washing-up liquid bottle and put in some dried beans. Then push a stick into the neck of the bottle and tape it so that it fits tightly. Paint the bottle with acrylic paint. Now you can shake and rattle even louder!

Shoe-box Guitar

It is quick and easy to make your own simple guitar.

1 Cut a large round hole towards one end of the shoe-box lid. To make this easier, put a round object, approximately 8 cm in diameter on the inside of the lid and draw around it. Then cut out the circle.

2 Tape the lid to the shoe box and cover the whole thing with sugar paper. Don't cover up the hole you have just made! Then use felt pens to decorate the box with colourful designs. Make a circular design around the hole.

3 Next make two bridges for the guitar strings. Score two 8-cm card squares in three places as shown. Then fold each square into a triangular stand and tape the edges together.

Attach a bridge to each end of the box with two strips of tape. Make sure that the bridges are in line with each other and the hole.

4 For best results, your four rubber bands should be slightly different sizes. Fit them carefully around the box and across the bridges. Check that each one is straight all around the box and not twisted. The biggest rubber band will be loosest and make the lowest sound, and the smallest and tightest will play the highest note. On a real guitar, the lowest string is at the top and the highest at the bottom.

Now you can hold up your guitar and pluck or strum the strings. You'll be surprised how good a shoe box can sound!

The guitar

The guitar is a very popular stringed instrument. An early form of guitar was probably brought to Spain by the Moors many hundreds of years ago. Classical composers have written music for the guitar, and many works of the classical masters, such as Bach and Chopin, have been arranged for the guitar. In this century, the greatest classical guitarist was Andrés Segovia (1893-1987), who improved the technique of guitar-playing. The classical guitar is often called an acoustic or a Spanish guitar. It is used in the Spanish flamenco, a lively form of dance and music, and is very popular with folk singers. Chords can be played by strumming all the strings at once. Single notes can be played by plucking one string at a time, often using a plectrum. Rock groups prefer the electric guitar, which sends the sound through an amplifier and can produce more sounds than an acoustic guitar.

Pop Star

Follow these instructions to make your own pop star drummer.

1 Use a large plastic bottle for the head. A bottle with a flat front and back is ideal. Find a rod or tube that fits into the opening, or make a thin cardboard tube about 50 cm long. Push it into the opening and tape the join. Then find or make a wider, slightly shorter tube for the body.

2 Then push a dowel rod through the thin tube to make the shoulders.

3 Thread a piece of thin rope through the body tube only, as shown. Carefully put the thinner tube inside the wider one - make sure that the rope doesn't get caught. To make hands, draw around your own hand and wrist twice on some card and cut the shapes out. Tape the hands to the rope arms.

4 Use felt scraps or paper to make two big eyes, eyebrows and a mouth. Stick them on the head. Add a nose, lots of woolly hair and a headband. You can also add some jewellery.

5 Dress him in a jazzy shirt. Pull the arms and hands through the sleeves. Button up the sleeves and collar.

6 To make a drumstick, twist some tissue paper into a ball and stick it onto a straw. Make two and glue the straws inside the hands. If you want to be able to control the drumsticks, tie a thin cane to the back of each hand with string. You will need another person to control the head if you are going to work the hands.

Now all your pop star needs is a drum kit! You can find out how to make your own drum on the next page. Now you've got the drummer, why not make a whole pop group?

Rock music

Rock is pop music with a heavy beat. It came from the American rock 'n' roll music of the 1950s. Rock with a very strong, loud beat is sometimes called heavy metal. The most important instrument in many rock bands is the electric guitar, and there are often three guitarists. The lead guitar plays the main tune, the rhythm guitar plays the backing, and the bass guitar adds the lower notes. The band's drummer plays three types of drums, as well as the cymbals. The big bass drum is played with the foot, while the tenor drums and smaller side drums are struck with drumsticks. Many bands add keyboards — electric organ, piano or synthesizer.

The first great rock 'n' roll star was Elvis Presley. His records sold millions in the 1950s and 60s.

Drum Away

1 You can use any round container for your drum. A deep biscuit tin will make a big drum and a loud noise! If you want a smaller drum, a cocoa tin will do.

2 Take off the lid — we are going to replace it with a drum skin. The best thing to use for this is cellophane. Stand the biscuit tin on the cellophane and cut a large square around it. Make sure that the cellophane overlaps the tin by 5 cm all the way round.

3 Spread the cellophane over the open end of the tin, pull it tight all the way round, and make folds around the sides to get a tight fit. When the drum skin is taut, secure it with a rubber band. Then put parcel tape around the edges.

4 To decorate your drum, measure the circumference of the tin and cut a piece of red felt long enough and wide enough to go around it. Allow a bit of extra length so that you can make a neat seam. Glue the felt all around the tin.

5 Cut strips of gold braid and stick them all around the drum as shown.

The kettledrum

Drums come in all sizes, and one of the biggest is the kettledrum, or timpano. This is different from all other drums in one important way. It is the only drum that can be tuned to make a definite note. Most symphony orchestras use at least three kettledrums. The skin of a kettledrum is stretched over a ring that is attached to a metal bowl. Some timpani are tuned by tightening or loosening screws around the top of the drum. Others are tuned by pressing a foot pedal and they are played using two sticks with soft heads.

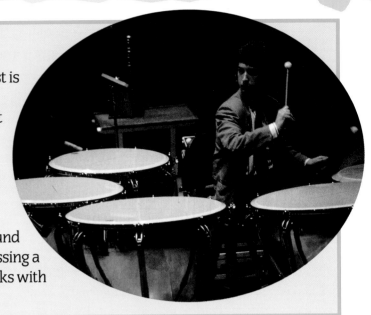

6 Cut two narrow strips of blue felt to go around the top and bottom of the drum. Glue them in position so that they cover the ends of the braid.

7 You can make different drumsticks by winding tape, string or felt around one end of a dowel rod or bamboo stick. You can also stick a bead or cork to the end of a stick. Each stick will make a different sound on your drum. Don't play too hard or you might break the drum skin.

Kazoo Band

YOU WILL NEED:
- ✔ toilet-roll tubes
- ✔ kitchen-paper rolls
- ✔ greaseproof paper
- ✔ rubber bands
- ✔ poster paint
- ✔ brushes

Make a set of kazoos in different sizes. Then you could get together with some friends and form a kazoo band.

1 Paint each tube a different colour. When this undercoat is dry, add colourful patterns.

2 When the paint is dry, cover one end of each tube with a piece of greaseproof paper, 12-cm square. Hold it in place with a rubber band.

3 For your kazoo performance, hum or sing into the open end of the tube. A longer tube will make a deeper sound. If you have enough people for a band, the longer kazoos could make a background hum while the shorter kazoos play a tune.

4 As a variation, you could make three holes in the tube of your kazoo with the point of a pencil. When you cover and uncover the finger holes as you hum, your kazoo will make a different sound.

Kazoos and clarinets

The kazoo is a very simple musical instrument. A metal or plastic kazoo has a piece of thin paper covering a hole. This vibrates when the player hums or sings into the blow hole and a note is produced. Our own home-made kazoo works in the same way.

Woodwind instruments work in a similar way. The clarinet (left), for example, has a reed in its mouthpiece, which vibrates against a slot. The reed is usually made from natural cane, or sometimes plastic, or metal. The vibration produces the sound, which is changed by pressing keys that cover holes in the tube.

Ping-pong Conductor

Introducing the conductor of the ping-pong orchestra...

YOU WILL NEED:
✔ ping-pong balls ✔ wool ✔ fabric scraps ✔ string
✔ dowel rod ✔ toothpick ✔ strong glue ✔ felt pens
✔ thin white card ✔ 1 garden rod for each musician
✔ black and white felt ✔ masking tape ✔ scissors
✔ pencil sharpener

1 The conductor's head is made from a ping-pong ball. Draw on the eyes, nose and mouth with felt pen. Stick on some wool hair and a felt moustache.

2 Sharpen a 30-cm-long dowel rod with a pencil sharpener and carefully push the pointed end into the bottom of the ping-pong head.

3 Cut a piece of string long enough for two arms. Tie and tape the middle of the string around the rod as shown. Draw four simple hand shapes onto white felt and cut them out.

4 The toothpick will be the conductor's baton, and you will use the garden rod to work the conductor. Place the toothpick and the rod between the two right-hand shapes, as shown, and stick them on. Then glue the hand shapes together and onto the string. Glue the left-hand shapes onto the other arm.

5 Roll two pieces of white card around a pencil to make shirt sleeves. Fit the tubes over the arms and tape them with masking tape.

6 A square of black felt or fabric makes the conductor's jacket. Cut out a small neck hole in the centre of the square, and stick the jacket to the dowel rod at the neck with masking tape.

7 Cut out a shirt front from white card. Add a black felt bow tie. Glue the shirt to the front of the jacket.

8 To work the conductor, hold his body in your left hand and the rod controlling the baton in your right hand. You could create a ping-pong orchestra to conduct by making musicians in the same way as the conductor. Why not make some musical instruments for them to play?

Conducting the orchestra

Imagine standing in front of 100 musicians and waving a small wooden stick to help them play a complicated piece of music in harmony. This is the job of the orchestral conductor, who must learn an amazing number of notes for every piece of music he conducts. His first task is to use his stick, called a baton, to beat time so that everyone plays at the right tempo. Music is divided into bars containing a number of beats, and the movement of the conductor's baton shows these beats. The conductor may use his other hand to signal to different sections of the orchestra. He may use both hands and even his whole body to show how loudly or quietly a passage should be played.

Hosepipe Panpipes

YOU WILL NEED:
- 132 cm of hosepipe
- cloth tape (coloured)
- strong glue
- plasticine

!

1 Ask an adult to cut the hosepipe into eight pieces. The first piece should be 20 cm long, the next 19 cm, the next 18 cm, and so on. The eighth piece will be 13 cm. *(If the hosepipe is curled up, soak it in warm water first.)*

2 Decorate the pipes with pieces of coloured cloth tape.

3 Assemble the pipes in order of size as shown. Wind a strip of cloth tape around one end of the pipes, and another strip around the other end.

4 Roll pieces of plasticine into plugs that will fit inside the panpipes. Put a plug in the bottom of each pipe so that no air can get in. Blow across the top end of each pipe. If you want to make the sound of a pipe higher, push the plug higher up into the pipe with a rod.

Pipes

Panpipes date back over 2,000 years, and ancient examples have been found in most parts of the world. Throughout this time, they have been made out of many different materials - stone, clay, wood, cane, plastic and metal. The instrument's name comes from an ancient Greek legend, in which the god Pan used a bundle of reeds to make music.

The idea for the oldest keyboard instrument, the organ (right), came from the panpipes. The first organ was the hydraulus, or water organ, invented in Alexandria in about 250 BC. Air was pumped through the organ's pipes by forcing water into a drum. The Roman emperor Nero (AD 37-68) played this instrument.

Scottish bagpipes use a different method. A windbag is filled with air from the piper's mouth, and arm pressure on the bag forces the air through the pipes.

To play the panpipes, you blow across the top of them, rather than down into them.

Thumb Piano

1 Use a rectangular piece of plywood, 15 cm x 20 cm and at least 15 mm thick, for the board of the piano. Smooth the edges of the plywood with sandpaper.

2 Ask an adult to cut a 2-cm wide strip of wood, to fit across the width of the board. Again, smooth the edges with sandpaper.

3 Place 4 lolly sticks at one end of the board so that they stick out over the edge at different lengths. Put the strip of wood over the sticks and press down to hold them in place. Now try twanging the sticks with your thumb. Move the sticks and the strip of wood until you are happy with the sound. Then tack them down in their positions on the board.

4 Now you need to nail down the strip of wood. Ask an adult to hammer the nails through the strip and into the board. First put a nail at each end of the strip. Check the position of the lolly sticks again. Then hammer three nails in between the sticks.

5 Use poster paints to decorate the board with African designs. When the paint is dry, varnish the wood.

To play your thumb piano, hold it in both hands, or at the edge of a table, and twang the ends of the sticks with your thumbs. You'll soon be making your own African rhythm.

The African sansa

The sansa, or thumb piano, is a traditional African instrument. It is made of a number of metal or cane strips fixed to a decorated wooden board or box. There are from 8 to over 20 strips, or tongues, on each box. These are plucked with the fingers or thumbs while holding the sansa in the hands or on the lap. The tongues make a twanging or buzzing sound. Sometimes the sansa is put into the shell of a large gourd — a fruit — to make it louder. The sansa is played as a solo instrument, in groups, or with other instruments.

Pop-up Singer

1 For your pop-up card, fold the sheet of paper in half lengthways, and then in half again. Make sharp creases.

YOU WILL NEED:
- ✔ *A3 sheet of cartridge paper or thin card*
- ✔ *pencil* ✔ *felt pens* ✔ *ruler* ✔ *craft knife*
- ✔ *cutting board* ✔ *scissors*

2 Unfold the sheet. Draw a line 7 cm from the bottom edge of the paper. The line should be 12 cm long and in the middle of the sheet, i.e. 6 cm either side of the centrefold. Place the sheet on a cutting board and ask an adult to cut along the line with a craft knife.

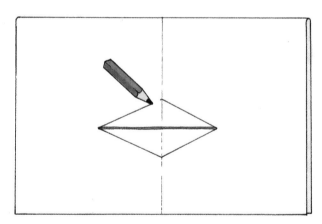

3 Make pencil marks on the centrefold, 3 cm below and above the middle of the slit. Draw 4 lines in a diamond shape, as shown in the drawing. Ask an adult to score the lines by going over them with the tip of a pair of scissors.

4 Now you can make the pop-up mouth. Fold the paper in half again. Hold the half of the diamond above the slit and, while closing the card slightly, pull it out and fold it upwards along the scored lines. Close the card with the top half of the mouth open. Then do the same with the bottom half of the diamond, and close the card with the whole mouth open.

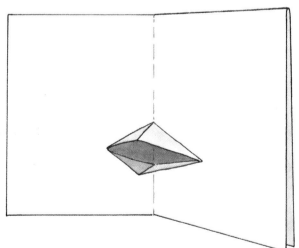

5 Open the card and draw a face around the mouth. Shade the inside of the mouth and paint the lips red. Add the eyes, nose and hair. You can copy this singer or draw your own favourite star.

6 Finally, you could draw a picture on the front of the card. Why not make some invitations for your very own karaoke party?

Singing voices

When we sing, we use our voice as a musical instrument. Women's voices are usually higher than men's, but they are not all the same. A high female voice is called soprano; a middle voice, mezzo-soprano; and a low voice, contralto (alto). A high male voice is called tenor; a middle, baritone; and a low, bass. Middle voices are the most common. Teachers build on a singer's natural gifts, and there are many methods of voice training. Some involve singing scales and exercises, while others concentrate more on singing actual songs.

Bottle Xylophone

1 Collect eight identical glass bottles. Arrange the bottles in a row and pour a different amount of water into each one.

2 If you tap the bottles with a pencil, you will hear that each one makes a different sound. Put the bottles in order, from the lowest note to the highest, and you have a simple bottle xylophone!

3 Do you know the scale "do, re, mi, fa, so, la, ti, do"? If not, you could ask an adult to help. Fill all the bottles nearly to the neck. Take the first bottle and call it "do". Pour a small amount of water out of the second bottle until it sounds like "re". Pour more out of the third bottle to make "mi" and so on.

4 When you have finished all eight bottles, you could label each one. Then close the bottles with screw tops or corks.

5 You can play your xylophone with one or two mallets. To make a mallet, sharpen the tip of a dowel rod with a pencil sharpener and glue a wooden bead on top. You can vary the sound by striking the bottles with different mallets. Try fixing a metal nut to a bamboo stick — but don't hit too hard with it!

Xylophones

The xylophone is a set of wooden bars that are struck with mallets. The bars are arranged on a frame in the order of the notes they play. The longer or thicker the bar, the lower the sound it makes. Xylophones are common in Africa, where the huge log xylophone is played by two or three musicians. The simple leg xylophone is made of a number of logs resting on the player's outstretched legs, while another type has neck-straps so that it can be carried about as it is played. The marimba of Central America has resonators beneath the bars to make it sound louder and deeper.

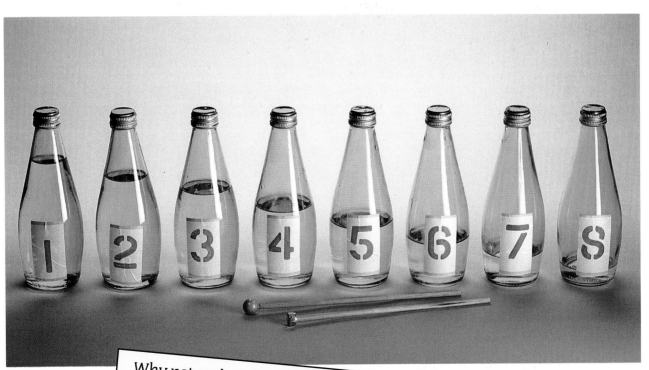

Why not make up your own piece of music on the bottle xylophone? Get together with some friends and play some music on your home-made instruments. You could even record your compositions on tape!

The Orchestra

There are several different layouts for an orchestra. Here is one example.

Strings

The string section is the heart of a symphony orchestra, containing more than half the musicians. There are more violins than any other instrument, usually as many as 30 or more. They are divided into two groups: the first and second violins. The first violins play the highest pitched music, and the first violinist is the leader of the orchestra. In addition, there are about 10 violas, 10 cellos and eight double basses. Sometimes there are one or more harps, a piano, or a harpsichord.

Brass

Two to four trumpets and four to eight French horns play the higher brass parts. Two to four trombones and one tuba play the lower parts. Sometimes saxophones are added. The brass section can play more loudly than the rest of the orchestra put together.

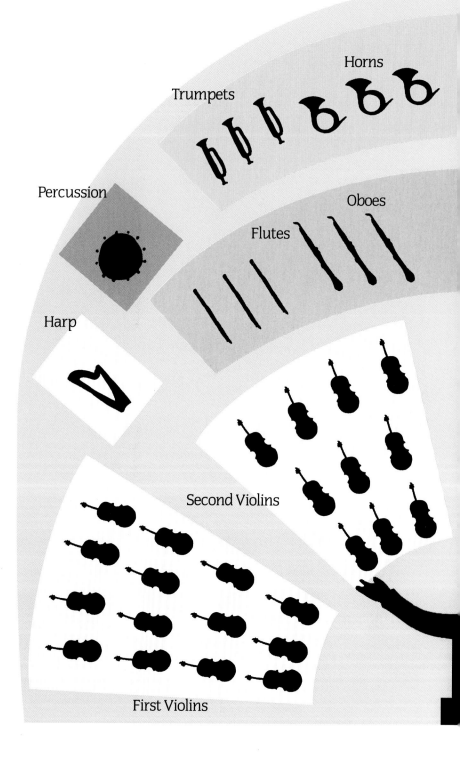

Horns

Trumpets

Percussion

Oboes

Flutes

Harp

Second Violins

First Violins

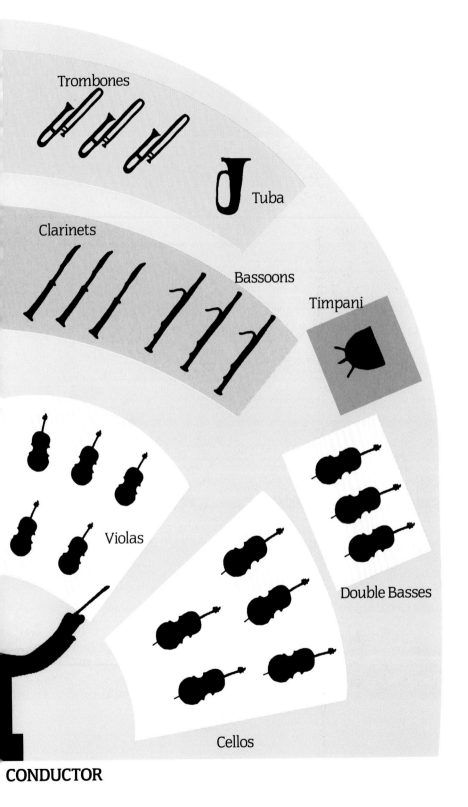

Trombones

Tuba

Clarinets

Bassoons

Timpani

Violas

Double Basses

Cellos

CONDUCTOR

Woodwind

In this section there are usually two to four flutes, oboes, clarinets, and bassoons. If needed, the woodwind musicians play other instruments too. A flautist (flute player) may change to the smaller piccolo, an oboist to the English horn, a clarinetist to the bass clarinet, and a bassoonist to the larger contrabassoon.

Percussion

This section includes any instrument that you can strike, rattle or shake. It normally includes two or more timpani (kettledrums), cymbals, a bass drum, snare drum, xylophone, and triangle. There might also be bells, a gong or a tambourine.

STRINGS

WOODWIND

BRASS

PERCUSSION

Glossary

acoustic guitar - often called a Spanish or classical guitar.

bar - a group of beats in a piece of music.

baritone - a middle male voice.

bass - a low male voice.

bass drum - a big drum with a low sound.

baton - a conductor's small wooden stick.

beat - the basic unit of rhythm in music, usually grouped in twos, threes or fours.

castanets - curved pieces of wood that are held between the fingers and thumb and clicked together.

contralto - a low female voice.

cymbals - circular metal discs, usually brass, that make a loud noise when they are clashed together or struck with a stick.

flamenco - a lively form of Spanish dance music.

gourd - a large fruit with a shell.

hydraulus - a water organ.

idiophones - instruments made of materials that naturally make a sound when struck or shaken, such as maracas.

karaoke - an entertainment in which people sing to a recorded backing.

kazoo - a simple instrument containing a thin piece of paper that vibrates with a buzzing sound when the player hums into it.

kettledrum - a big drum that can be tuned to make a definite note.

Latin America - areas of the Americas where Spanish or Portuguese are spoken — South and Central America, Mexico and certain Caribbean islands.

maracas - instruments that you shake to make a rattling sound.

marimba - a Latin American xylophone with resonators that makes a deep, rich sound.

membrane - a thin sheet, such as the skin of a drum or the paper that vibrates in a kazoo.

mezzo-soprano - a middle female voice.

Moors - a Muslim people of North Africa.

panpipes - a number of reeds or whistles of different lengths bound together.

percussion instrument - a musical instrument that makes a sound when it is struck, rattled or shaken.

plectrum - a small piece of plastic that guitarists sometimes use to pluck or strum the strings.

reed - a thin piece of cane, metal or plastic in the mouthpiece of wind instruments, that vibrates to produce sound.

resonator - anything that increases the richness of sound, such as the gourds or hollow pieces of wood or metal beneath the bars of a marimba.

sansa - an African thumb piano.

scale - a group of notes in order going up or down.

Useful Websites

www.kidsdomain.com/ craft provides step-by-step instructions and photographs for a range of themed craft activities.

www.crafts4kids.com features a variety of craft projects from around the world. Step-by-step instructions are given, as well as printable templates.

Places to visit
United Kingdom

The Musical Museum
368 High Street
Brentford, Middlesex
TW8 OBD
www.musicalmuseum.co.uk

Finchcocks Living Museum of Music
Goudhurst, Kent
www.finchcocks.co.uk

Australia

Darnum Musical Village
Cloverlea Road
Darnum
VIC
3822

Callaway Centre
School of Music
The University of Western Australia
Nedland, WA
www.arts.uwa.edu.au/ circme

Note to parents and teachers
Every effort has been made by the Publishers to ensure that these websites are suitable for children; that they are of the highest educational value, and that they contain no inappropriate or offensive material. However, because of the nature of the Internet, it is impossible to guarantee that the contents of these sites will not be altered. We strongly advise that Internet access is supervised by a responsible adult.

Index

Africa 23, 27

Bach, Johann Sebastian 11
bagpipes 21
bass clarinet 28
bass drum 13, 29, 30
bassoon 28
bells 29
brass 28

castanets 9, 30
cello 28
Central America 27
Chopin, Fryderyk 11
clarinet 17, 28
conductor 19
contrabassoon 28
cymbals 9, 13, 29, 30

dance 9, 11
double bass 28
drums 13

electric guitar 11, 13
English horn 28

flamenco 11, 30
flute 28
French horn 29

gong 29
guitar 11, 30

harp 28
harpsichord 28
heavy metal 13

idiophones 9, 30

kazoo 17, 30
kettledrum 15, 30
keyboards 13

Latin America 7, 9, 30

maracas 9, 30
marimba 27, 30

oboe 28
orchestra 15, 19, 28
organ 13, 21

Pan 21
panpipes 21, 30
percussion 7, 29, 30

piano 13, 28
piccolo 28
pop groups 7, 9

reed 17
rock groups 11
rock music 13

sansa 23, 30
saxophone 29
Segovia, Andrés 11
side drum 13, 30
singing 25
snare drum 29, 30
Spain 7, 11
strings 28
synthesizer 13, 30

tambourine 7, 29
tenor drum 13, 30
timpani 15, 29, 30

triangle 9, 29, 30
trombone 29
trumpet 29
tuba 29

viola 28
violin 28
voices 25

water organ 21, 30
woodwind 17, 29

xylophone 9, 27, 29

Additional photographs:
Alan Hutchison Library 23;
Clive Barda - P.A.L. 16-17;
Redferns 15, 19, title page;
Tony Stone Worldwide 7;
Zefa Picture Library 11, 13,
21, 25, 27